# A Joyful Miracle

*How I made my father's death a joyful miracle
and how you can plan for this too*

by
Nancy A. Waldron

Everything

is in

Divine Order

**Dedicated to my father**

Walter Hermann Henrich Otte
April 14, 1907 to October 6, 1998


**From your loving daughter**

Nancy A. (Otte) Waldron
November 12, 1940 to Present

# Table of Contents

# Introduction

In the year 2000, the first edition of *A Joyful Miracle* was written with the thought of honoring my Father, the journey we had together, and how his death became a joyful miracle for me. I am an avid reader, and at the time I looked around for happy "how-to" books about the dying process and found few. I thought how wonderful it would be if someone wrote a book about the joyful miracles which occur to those who choose to be "consciously aware" during the ordinary person's death process. Then I thought, why don't I write about Daddy's death?

I'm guessing each member of my family had a different experience during Daddy's death, just as we each had different experiences during his life. Writing about mine helped me to deepen my experience of the joyful miracles which occurred.

I have written what is meaningful to me about his death. I wanted to honor the fact that he had such an impact on my life by dying. His death changed my outer life, as well as my inner life. I stopped doing many of the things I was doing in the past, to give myself the opportunity to go deeper within myself, to explore what spiritual meaning Daddy had to me and I to him. Because of this, I'm keenly aware of every aspect of life and I live it much more fully and joyfully.

I also wanted to write about the death process for those who are afraid of their own feelings about death or any part of the dying process. For me, it has been one of the most uniquely joyful experiences of my life. Had I been lost in my own grief, I would have missed so much.

For myself, grieving over Daddy's death was very short. I felt complete with Daddy and had no unfinished business. I think about him occasionally and feel like he is close in spirit. It has allowed me to become much more present to my everyday life. By being fully present in each moment, I cannot focus on anything except what is going on right now. This eliminates the past and future movies of "what should have been" or what "could be" that used to run in my mind.

Being in the "now" is one of the major keys to my inner joy. I am able to do this most of the time, and I am so blessed. I feel wonderful inside when I am able to stay in the moment, and it is a constant inspiration.

By writing I offer the inner part of my heart and trust that my experience will be of some comfort or I will have helped by telling you the steps I followed. May my words fill you and those you love with infinite blessings.

In 2017, this second edition is written with the thought of continuing to honor all the above things, and imparting the certainty that Spirit is with us every moment of every day. My life is dedicated to Spirit, and because of that it is so much richer, and has a rareness because I allow Spirit in everything.

The manner in which my life has changed and unfolded is remarkable. The conscious knowing is with me all the time, and guides my every thought, word, and action.

The update for the second edition was written because my soul has expanded in ways I never expected and continues to expand every day.

I encourage you to allow Spirit everywhere in your life; ask for Spirit's help every minute of every day.

You are *love* in life and in death, in all the phases and stages in between and beyond. I encourage you to hold that as the highest goal for yourself and as your gift to those around you.

Always you the human, you the Spirit, are loved beyond measure.

*Nancy A. Waldron*

## CHAPTER 1
# Advance Preparation of the Spirit

As I watched the life slowly flow out of my father at 8:35 a.m. the morning of October 6, 1998, I felt strangely calm and peaceful. I marveled that I could feel so calm as I heard the gurgling sound in his lungs stop and I watched him become still. I thought about this calmness at the time and have given considerable thought to it since.

I believe my experience during his illness and death was easier because of the steps I took to prepare. I feel compelled to share it with those who may need a way to face themselves before such a life changing event. Years ago, I was a person who didn't think I could stand it if my father died. I felt like I would go to pieces as the loss would be so great.

I asked his Spirit not to leave his body at a couple of points in my life when I believe he had the opportunity to make his transition. I had the conscious awareness, or knowing, that if I asked, it could make a difference in him staying a while longer.

I define "conscious awareness" as choosing to look at, and be aware of, as many meanings as possible in all that happens, and what my connection is to Spirit. My definition of "unconscious awareness" is that whatever happens I choose not to look at it or be aware of any but the most obvious meaning in it. I define "Spirit" as God or God Force or Higher Power; in other words, that Divine energy that flows to, through, and from me.

For most of my life I called my father "Daddy" until the last two or three years when I started calling him "Dad." This helped move him a little further from my heart so I wouldn't hurt so badly when he was gone. It helped while he was here, but he again became "Daddy" when he was gone.

I was born in Oklahoma, lived the early part of my life on a small farm, by a small town, then just before I entered my teen years moved to Colorado. Our family life was pretty simple. We all worked together in the family unit every day, went to town on Saturday, and to church on Sunday. God, the land, and the weather were all very important parts of life for our family, especially for my father. When I graduated from high school, I moved to Los Angeles, California, went to work for the federal government, married a Los Angeles police officer, and lived there for many years. In 1988, we moved to Northern California just south of Mt. Shasta. I tell you these things so that you know I have a rather simple background and yet have had some profound experiences during my life.

Years ago, while I was visiting the folks (I always called my mother and father "the folks"), we all watched the movie, *Out on a Limb*, with Shirley MacLaine. She has a book by the same title. In this movie, Shirley MacLaine tells the story of how her spiritual experiences unfolded and she went from being a skeptic to being immersed in Spirit. It tells how she went from place to place and found different parts of her spiritual self, and ultimately ended up in Peru in the Mantaro River Valley having experiences with off-planet beings. Her experiences changed her life completely and it helped change humanity. This movie was so impactful for me; it frightened me and challenged me. It frightened me because I had the feeling it might be true, and it challenged me to explore more.

During the movie, Mother innocently made the comment to me that I could do that, meaning that I could go to Peru and hike around. For me it was much more than that, and I "knew" with certainty that I would go to Peru although I did not know when. This was my first "conscious awareness" of an ordinary miracle.

2

Bill, my husband, and I went to Peru in 1996 and experienced the "much more." I did not have a focus as to what that "much more" would be when we first watched *Out on a Limb*. My awareness of the special miracles during Daddy's death, as well as the ordinary miracles I experienced, is part of the "much more." "Special miracles" involved my father's validation of Spirit's work through me and him, as well as our conversations about them. Ordinary miracles involved the flow of timing, people and events, and the order in which things happened.

After seeing that movie, I intensified my efforts for the next few years to understand death and to also have more meaning in my life by reading books, taking classes, attending spiritual seminars, and discussing my thoughts and feelings with various people. A friend who is a Medium played a major part in changing my awareness by sharing her actual experiences. She connects with Spirits every day and they give her information on all kinds of things, like relationships, weather, earthquakes, spiritual ethics, values, and laws, government, and so forth. The breadth and depth of her information was astounding. She would give me information that no one could have known and then expound on the meaning for my life and other's lives. When I learned to understand why something I didn't like had happened from a spiritual perspective, I no longer viewed experiences as "bad," but rather as opportunities for spiritual growth. What I came to believe – first with my head and then slowly with my heart – is that there really is no death in terms of the Spirit. There is only death in terms of the physical body. I now view death as a birth into the nonphysical or Spirit world.

The strength of my belief in nonphysical life comes from my own research, observations, and personal experience.

Daddy helped birth me into the physical, and now I was to help birth him into the nonphysical. There are three main events in my life which are significant in some way, that unfolded as each of these took place: the first is birth, the second is marriage, and the third is death. I will share my experience of how these all seem to connect during Daddy's illness and death.

In January 1998, a friend knew of my interest in life after death and taped a TV program of James Van Praagh when he was on the Larry King Live Show. He wrote *Talking With Heaven* which Bill and I immediately purchased and read. The manner in which James Van Praagh conducted himself and the integrity he exhibited while he was talking to people on the telephone left little room for doubt about nonphysical life. I believe it profoundly affected my father's death and my family's handling of it. I made a copy of the TV program segment to show to all those who were willing to view it.

I showed it to my parents and my sisters while I was visiting in June 1998. Although Daddy dozed off, afterwards he asked me some questions about the process and I explained it. I believe that if a person wants to, he/she receives the information even though he/she may fall asleep. Daddy got a look on his face like he already knew what it was as he said: "I thought that's what it was. I sure hope it's true. Thank you, Sweetie." I had sent Daddy a couple of other books to read along the lines of life after death prior to this and had talked with him at other times about my beliefs.

June of 1998 was the beginning of my awareness of his illness when Bill and I took a trip to Colorado to see my folks. Mother needed a rest as she was a tremendously devoted caregiver for Daddy. My Dad had colon cancer in the late 1980's and had to have a colostomy. He was having accidents more frequently, which resulted in stress for Mother and her having more to do. She also felt tied down, wanting to be with him all day as he wasn't too stable on his feet, yet needing some time to herself.

We were excited about taking Daddy over to Silverton, Colorado, where he had some property and where we all loved to go. We had a wonderful trip and as usual when we three were together, we experienced a "high." By "high" I mean that there is such a feeling of love that flows between us with lots of jokes, laughter, sensitivity to one another's feelings without words, appreciation of the beauty of nature, and God's hand in all - that harmony just flows. Some people would call it intuition or being on the same wavelength or being in tune with each other; whatever it is called, it feels "divinely inspired" to me.

In life, there are some people with whom I intuitively know I have a connection that doesn't require words, that somehow goes beyond the relationship apparent on the surface of life. With these people, I immediately feel a closeness that doesn't require any of the usual getting acquainted devices. Daddy was one of these people for me, and for many, whether they had known him all his life or just met him. People said that he never met a stranger.

On the trip, Daddy did fine. He rode up front until his legs went to sleep and then we fixed him a place in the backseat so he could stretch out in comfort. He was having problems with his hips, knees, and back. The circulation in his legs being cut off when he sat in any one position for too long. As he put it, from the waist down he was no good. He was a big man: 6'4" tall and weighed over 200 pounds, with big bone structure.

We looked at the property Daddy gifted to me while we were there. Each day we drove around remembering our various trips. I am the adventurous one in the family and love the mountains. While we were up at Animas Forks, elevation around 11,000 feet, I felt like something more was wrong with Daddy's body than his lower part. He got out of the car, leaned against it looking pale, and commented that he was short of breath. We immediately got in the car and drove back to Silverton, elevation 9,000 feet. He felt better and did not mention any further discomfort during the trip. We all came back from the trip feeling blessed. I had the sense that this was the last trip we would be taking together, and I was happy that I had given myself this time alone with him. If I had never seen him again, I knew I would be fine. We gave so much love to each other during that trip to the place we all loved. It was his last trip, and our last trip to Silverton.

We returned to our Northern California home the latter part of June, and on July 9 we received a call that Daddy had nine spots on his lungs and they were cancerous. I knew when we received that call that it was the beginning of the end.

I had started my grieving process a couple of years before, well in advance of his death. For a while I wrote him many letters on my computer, the things I loved and didn't love about him. At times, I cried when I wrote to him, no matter what the letter was about. I did not mail any of these letters. I handwrote and mailed one letter in which I told him how much I loved him, how precious he was to me, and how much I would miss him when he was gone.

At a certain point, I was able to switch from writing to just thinking and resolving things in my mind. This served to speed up my processing time considerably as I became physically tired writing on my computer for long periods. I thought about our life together, grieved for what we had missed, and celebrated what we had shared. They were all happy tears because I had such a deep "conscious awareness" of our spiritual experience in our life journey together.

I began telling Bill my thoughts which helped Bill and I verbalize our grief and joy, and served to draw us closer. Bill shared that he felt like Daddy was his father also, and that this was a profound loss for him. He had never shared that thought with me before, and it touches me deeply that he loved Daddy that much. It also gave me an understanding why we three had such a wonderful feeling when we were together. We were a family within a family. I experience these same feelings with our three children now. I feel such profound joy to have so many avenues for expression and feelings of love, and to be "consciously aware" of them.

While I grieved the loss of the rare connection that I felt Daddy and I had with each other, there were also things that I did not like about my father. I found many surprise gifts for my heart through writing and thinking about the things I did not like about him. I learned that by not getting what I wanted from him

I discovered what I had really wanted, and saw in some cases where I had gotten it at a much later point in my life than when I first wanted it. I also saw that if I had gotten it at the time I wanted it, I wouldn't have made the efforts I did to grow and change. I then forgave him for being unable to give me what I wanted and forgave myself for holding onto the anger and withholding my love from him at times.

After forgiveness came such a peaceful feeling along with the knowledge that the lesson was "divinely inspired" to expand my conscious understanding of love through the relationship of myself and Daddy. With each revelation, I experienced a lightness that occurred within my physical body. Ultimately, my love for everyone was strengthened as well as my connection with God. I am so grateful for the joy and gratitude I experience by allowing myself to really feel all of these things. For so many years I avoided "feeling" beyond a surface level. In the past, I covered my genuine needs with humor or attempted to control my exterior world rather than my inner self.

This pattern became the way I handled all people in my life. Some years ago, when I started making inner emotional shifts, I adjusted my relationship with people least close to me first and then those closest to my heart. Some people never clear all of the emotional baggage they carry. Then, when a loved one dies, they have to deal with it for years afterward. I did not want to be one of those people. For me it is like making New Year's resolutions. I do whatever I need to do as soon as I become aware of it so I don't need to make New Year's resolutions. Nothing is left undone with "conscious awareness."

After I received the call that he had nine cancerous spots on his lung, I wrote out his obituary, an outline of the funeral service, rewrote a poem he had sent me years ago, found a special picture of him I had saved, and wrote a thank you note for the family to send after his death and funeral. Through doing these things I lived his death in advance, and I celebrated and grieved each step of the way. I meditated daily and prayed frequently.

As I wrote the obituary I would picture him in the wheat fields or at various organizational meetings where I accompanied him and grieved that I would not be doing things with him anymore, and celebrated that I had been able to share such a rich life with him. I grieved for the occasions I had missed being with him because I lived so far away and celebrated that it made our times together so much more joyful.

I grieved for the history of our similar interests and that I would have no one to talk with now; i.e., the trips where he could tell me everyone's background from his home to the farm 150 miles east. I celebrated that I witnessed his magnificent memory - I called it an "audio" memory, similar to a photographic memory, in that he recorded, recalled, and repeated in detail everything he heard. He had an eighth-grade education, but a Ph.D. in experience. I grieved the loss of this fine being, and I celebrated that he had been a big part of my inner life.

I didn't spend days on end crying; I would set aside a time each day, depending upon my schedule, dedicated to grieving/ celebrating, and the rest of the day I went about my normal activities. Most days I didn't grieve at all, but found a calm inner happiness. If I found myself having trouble pulling out of the grieving process. I would call my friends with whom I have wonderful open-heart relationships, and talk with them. This grieving and celebrating process has been one of the happiest and most freeing times of my life. After every grieving session, I would feel so much better, lighter, and more consciously aware of the impact Daddy had in my life, and it would move me right into feeling joyful and grateful. This powerful process is one I recommend. It flowed over into all areas of my life and continues to expand into all of my relationships.

I encourage the following actions as advance preparations:

- Meditate daily
- Pray frequently
- Grieve/celebrate now
- Write now
- Talk now
- Forgive now
- Love now

# CHAPTER 2
## Enjoy Illness

Toward the end of July, x-rays revealed that Daddy now had eleven spots on his lungs which had grown larger. The doctor told him they could do surgery, chemotherapy, radiation, or let nature take its course, and then asked him what he wanted to do. Daddy said: "Well, I'm ninety-one years old and I've had a good life, why don't we just let nature take its course." This sounded so like Daddy to choose to keep his death simple, just like he had chosen to keep his life simple. On July 31, my sister. Barbara, called me and told me that the doctor gave Daddy from a few weeks to three months to live. I consider it a "Divine" gift that we had advance notice.

I immediately sat down and wrote letters to people around the world who knew Daddy and I felt would want to know about his impending death. I told them how long he had to live and that if they wanted to say or do anything for him before he died, I wanted them to have the opportunity to do so. I did not tell Daddy that I had done this until just before his death. Many people thanked me for notifying them in advance as they wanted to let him know the impact he had on their lives, either at some particular point or overall. It was very moving for me to witness the letters and calls he received to cheer him and, especially, to experience his joy for making a difference in so many people's lives.

Had I not done the outer work of genuinely searching, reading, attending spiritual seminars, and making like-minded friends, the inner work of meditating and, to a certain extent, reliving our life together, I believe I would have been devastated by Daddy's death and spent considerable time and energy grieving later.

Bill and I went to Colorado to see Daddy and Mother using the reason that it was their anniversary and we wanted to celebrate with them. Daddy was not told how long he had to live. It was decided that it was in his best interest not to put an arbitrary time limit on his life. Mother knew we were coming because a friend of ours let it slip to her, but Daddy didn't know. When we walked in and I went over to the bed to give him a kiss, he burst into tears and so did I. The love I felt flow between us was physically tangible to me. I am able to feel very fine energy vibrations and along with them usually come feelings with the thought of a color or colors. I felt like Daddy and I were filled with a radiant love while being enveloped in pink and gold twinkling lights whenever we hugged each other. Again, my "conscious awareness" of what I was feeling and the colors that came into my mind illuminated that moment for me.

By this time hospice was caring for him, he had a hospital bed at home, and different medical, and nonmedical people came to see to his needs. He was on morphine, but still getting out of bed some. He was able to be at the table for their 61st wedding anniversary celebration, taking pictures of the table, people, and all about the celebration, which he would later send as a surprise to everyone. That was his last party – their 61st wedding anniversary – I feel such joy that he gave so much of himself to Mother, our family, and friends. I was aware of each person and their relationship with Daddy at that party in a "conscious" way. I observed many details and nuances of expression that I would not have noticed before. Instead, I would have been focused on my own feelings rather than paying attention to anything else.

While we were in their home we talked about the usual family subjects, looked at old pictures, shared the mail that came, watched their favorite TV programs, and went over business things. I also helped do whatever necessary to assist with meals and his physical care. It was one of the most joyful and close times I have had with him. I had no unresolved issues within myself or between us. I believe he felt this special closeness also.

On the same day Mother and my sister, Barbara, who lives in the same city, both expressed the feeling that taking care of Daddy was getting to be too much. So, I felt the need to take action to assure that an alternate source of care was available before I went back to California. Mother, Barbara, and I discussed the hours that care would be needed. Barbara and I contacted two independent agencies who furnished licensed caregivers. One agency, who brought a three-ring binder with a contract, required a minimum numbers of hours work, and had an expensive hourly rate which didn't feel right to Mother. The other service had people available on an "as needed" basis, and we knew one of the references provided. This was the agency Mother chose, and she promised me she would try the service. She also said that Daddy wouldn't like it and wouldn't want it.

Every family has one member who takes on the more difficult tasks. I am that person in my family where my father was concerned. So just before I knew we were going to leave, I spoke with Daddy about needing to get some help at home both at night and at times during the day. I also told him that if he didn't want anyone in the home then maybe it would be better for him to consider going to a residential care center. It was one of the most difficult things I have done in my life.

I could feel his panic and fear at the thought of having someone come into his home or for him to leave his home. He said he didn't think they needed anyone in their home, that Mother and Barbara had been doing fine taking care of him. I told him what they had said to me. He asked me how I would feel if some stranger was going to come into my home and stay all night. He told me that he didn't want to go to a residential care center. I told him I never wanted him to get sick or have anyone come into his home or go to a residential care center or to have him die. I wanted him to live forever and for us to keep on going on trips and having fun together. Bill was in the room with me and we were all crying. Daddy could feel our love for him and that we were trying to assist for the good of everyone the best way we could. He agreed to have someone come into the home.

A couple of days later I told him we needed to go home and when we were going to leave. He didn't want us to leave. He told me he wished we could continue to stay there with him and I felt the same way. The night I told him goodbye, I felt a mixture of sadness and joy at the wonderful experiences we had shared. I didn't know if that would be the last time I saw him, so I told him how much I loved him and that I'd see him later or on the Other Side. He said: "Okay, Sweetie." It is that love between us which is a sacred gift I keep in my heart.

---

I recommend the following actions as this made things easier and more meaningful.

- Notify family and friends
- Spend time together
- Celebrate special events
- Be honest with yourself and each other
- Do the difficult things
- Express your deep feelings

## CHAPTER 3

# Nine Happy Days of Death

Mother called on Monday, September 28, to let me know that Daddy had fallen around 3:30 a.m., broken his leg, and was in the hospital. She said the doctor was going to operate on Wednesday and that she wanted me to come after the surgery to help. I woke up Tuesday morning knowing I needed to be with him and yet hesitating somewhat. I knew this was the end, and I didn't want to face losing him. I could see Spirit was making everything easier by moving him out of the home into the hospital where no family members had to care for him and where he could leave his body easily – an ordinary miracle.

On my way to a couple of errands, I stopped by to see a friend of mine and told her what had happened. Her first words were: "He's waiting for you." She confirmed what I knew in my heart. I arranged my flight for that evening. After I completed my plans, Barbara called and said she thought I had better come right away. I told her I had already made arrangements and gave her my flight arrival time. When she picked me up at the airport we went directly to the hospital to see Daddy.

When I walked into the hospital room and saw him I felt an immediate peace come over me and an inner calmness and strength that has stayed with me since. He was so glad to see me and apologized for falling and creating problems. I told him this gave me a chance to come and see him again. I stayed with him that night and each day thereafter.

The first night after Mother and Barbara left, I went immediately to the foot of Daddy's bed, put my fingers on each foot, and pictured brilliant white light coming from God entering Daddy's feet, going through his body and out the top of his head. I call this my "Light work." At the same time, I was picturing this, I asked God to help his body be free of pain and trauma, and to make his death easy and quick if this was his time to die. I did this periodically during each day. Each time it gave me a lighter feeling, and in some way, I sensed that I was helping Daddy.

Shortly after I arrived he developed a bladder infection and surgery was postponed. When I first heard that they were going to operate, my thought had been: "Why?" I consider this an ordinary miracle; Spirit knew what was best was no surgery and arranged an infection to postpone it. The doctors started him on an antibiotic and said to wait a few days to see how he was.

One afternoon when it was just the two of us, Daddy started talking to me about not wanting the surgery. He said it was just too big an uphill pull and he didn't have the strength to make it through the surgery and all that went with it. I told him I understood how he felt. that I would stay with him until he died and go part way with him. By part way, I mean that my Spirit would go with him as far as I could without leaving my physical body. Divine Beings on the Other Side would be there to welcome him and escort him the rest of the way, so that he was never alone. I also told him that I loved him and I would miss him so much when he was gone. It was joyful for me to allow him to freely talk about any part of the dying process or anything else that he wanted to. I gave myself a huge gift by opening my heart completely to him and being as totally "conscious" of every part of the process as I could be.

I've been with families when a member is dying and the person dying starts to talk about what they feel and the family members immediately deny all or part of the process, or are so focused on their own feelings they miss the great gifts. I used to do this; I wouldn't even go to funerals. I feel this makes it more difficult for the person dying and blocks the hearts of those participating in the process.

I told Daddy that I had been feeling the presence of Grandma (his mother), Grandpa (his father), Uncle Ernie (his brother), Uncle George (my mother's brother), Roscoe (a friend who died quite young), and Dopey (a dog we had as kids) around me for about two months and that I felt like they were waiting for him. He said he had been thinking about his mother and father a lot and he hoped he would see them again.

I told him I wanted to share with him all of the things I had prepared for his death. I went over the obituary, the funeral service, the poem, and even the thank you note with him. I made a list of the things he asked me to do for him and told him if I could I would do them or see that they were done. At one point when I was telling him about the funeral he got tears in his eyes. At that moment, I just kissed him on the cheek and ran my hand softly over his head to comfort him. It gave me such joy to feel I was comforting him and that we had the freedom to share the plans I had made for his funeral. There is nothing better than when someone is willing to receive the love you give as well as return it.

At Bill's birthday party in 1993, we had a professional photographer take pictures and there was one of Daddy waving his hand as if he was saying "so long." I had placed that picture in the death file I set up years ago. I had five copies enlarged and framed to give to Mother, my sisters, and my aunts after Daddy died. I showed one to him and he was so pleased, saying, "That's a good picture of me." He loved taking and giving pictures of everyone else, and I wanted to honor him in that way. Again, if I had avoided emotionally experiencing his death before it happened, I do not feel I would have had the awareness to prepare in advance.

After we finished going over everything about his death, the funeral, and the things he wanted done afterward, he seemed more peaceful. He thanked me for taking care of everything. I didn't have the presence of mind at the time to thank him for being so open, but I believe he knows my every thought since he died. He developed pneumonia over the weekend, wasn't eating, and generally slept more. I felt happy that I could really be there for him in ways meaningful to both of us, so it was not sad for me, but rather joyful. More ordinary miracles with Spirit helping him move closer to leaving his body by having pneumonia develop.

At times, his breathing would begin to speed up and be labored. I very slowly rubbed my hand down his chest, from his throat to his heart and said to him: "Slow it down, Daddy. Slow your breathing down." He would immediately slow his breathing rate and I would tell him how good he was doing and how proud I was of him. Other times I just held my hand over his lungs and pictured "light" expanding the cells in his lungs, and asked God to help him breathe better. Immediately his labored breathing would ease, and I was filled with the wonderful feeling of joy.

One afternoon I stood at the side of Daddy's bed silently sending him "Light," and I thought he was asleep because his eyes were closed and his breathing was even. In the middle of sending him light he said: "That's enough, Sweetie." I was shocked at the time, and I stopped and said: "OK," then sat down and read. Later, I thought about it and realized what a validation it was that he could sense what I was doing. This is one of the special miracles and a treasure I have tucked in my heart to cherish.

I noticed my touch brought him comfort and I felt such happiness that I could ease him in any way. I bathed his face with a cold washcloth or I rubbed lotion on his body or held his broken leg when the nurses turned him. I felt deep satisfaction when I did these things; somehow the silent communication we had between us fed my soul in ways I have only experienced a few times before in my life.

One of these times was when my uncle died and our family got together in a motel room to visit before the funeral. Filled with what I call "Divine Love," - I felt only love for all people and things, and so filled with a brilliant golden light that, in some ways, I felt like I was the light. At that moment, I "knew" what I was to do in certain situations in years to come. It is this same feeling I had all during the time I was taking care of Daddy, so focused on loving him that all sense of "self" disappeared and I became part of the whole, my "Divine self" connecting all. These I consider special miracles.

The doctors and I thought Daddy would die over the weekend, but he kept going. I discovered there was "Divine" purpose in this as I watched different people come to complete something with Daddy. He would appear to be sleeping while the family was in the room, but as soon as someone else came in, he awakened and was quite coherent and clear, visiting with each person. We would look at each other in amazement at this ordinary miracle.

A couple of days before Daddy died, I had the urge to talk to him about death. I asked him if he was afraid to die, and he said that he wasn't afraid to die, that he had had a good life and was ready to go. It wasn't so much what he said as the way he said it and the look he had on his face of acceptance and certainty. I loved that about Daddy; what he felt was genuine and his words matched his actions. He wasn't telling you one thing and doing another behind your back.

He told me that his dad had fallen, broken his leg, and been in the hospital thirteen days before he died on October 20. Barbara told me in August that she thought Daddy would die in October because he had followed his father's pattern throughout his life. She was correct.

The day before Daddy died, he had talked nonstop all day and been extremely restless wanting to get out of bed and go home. That night I had such a clear feeling that a dark heaviness from my toes to just above my hip joints was removed, that I noted it and thought it was connected to Daddy in some way. It was similar to heavy depression when the body feels weighted down because of emotion. When I woke up the next morning, the heaviness had lifted from the rest of my body, and I immediately noticed I felt lighter all over. Again, I had the thought that it was connected with Daddy in some way. To me, this was an ordinary miracle of Spirit demonstrating to me the pure connection I had with my father in a physical way.

When I walked in the next morning he was totally different and appeared to be in a deep sleep. The night nurse left and I was there with him alone. I kissed him, said good morning, and did my "Light work" with him and God. A little while later he opened his eyes, looked around, and said: "Good morning, Sweetie." I caressed his face and gave him a kiss. Then he went back to sleep.

Around 8:15 a.m., the nurse's assistant came in and we decided to give him a bath. I started bathing him, washing his face and neck when we noticed he was having trouble breathing. She said: "He's having trouble breathing." I looked at her and said with certainty: "He's going." I sat down and held his hand while his spirit left his body. I don't know how, but I was aware that his spirit was moving up his chest and out through the top of his head. I could see parts of him becoming still and see the color of his body change as this happened.

It is still amazing to me that I had the "awareness" to watch so closely what was going on with him physically. I remember my attention specifically being drawn to these things at the time, so much so that I could not look away. I equated the feelings I had the night before and the next morning to the process of the spirit leaving the body. I felt I had received the information of Daddy's death through my own body. I spoke to my family about it at the time, but didn't realize the significance of it until later. This was another "Divine" gift for me because I was "consciously aware," a special miracle.

As soon as I knew Daddy was dead, I called Bill, my mother and Barbara (who were already on their way to the hospital), and then my other sister, Patricia, to tell her I thought she should come to the hospital right away. The nurse came in, asked me if I was all right, and I told her I was fine. She told me she would get a doctor to "pronounce him." The hospital chaplain came in shortly to see if I needed anything and then my mother and sisters arrived.

I felt I had been honored in a big way to be the one with Daddy when he died. I found nothing about the rest of the process that disturbed me. I felt like celebrating that he was no longer in pain, that he had a short period of discomfort only at the end of his life, and that he had just slipped out quietly. It was so like Daddy not to make a fuss. I felt so joyful to have been with him to the end.

He was beside me when I was birthed into this world; I was beside him when he was birthed out of this world. He walked beside me down the aisle at my marriage to escort me to my husband; I walked beside him in Spirit to escort him to the Divine Beings waiting on the Other Side. Incredibly beautiful, touching special miracles for both of us.

After the other family members said goodbye to Daddy and left, I stayed with the body until the mortician came. A minister from my parents' church had come earlier and stayed with me. During the time we were waiting for the mortician we had the most wonderful visit, sharing what we had done in our lives and where we were presently. She shared that she was having a problem with her foot, and this led to my sharing about my husband's back problem being healed through nonmedical means with Spirit's assistance.

From the time I met this minister I felt a unique quality in her – a humility and genuine depth of caring. Her simplicity reminded me a lot of Daddy's simplicity. We had not planned to have her participate in the funeral ceremony, but we decided to because of the connection between her and Daddy. The afternoon before he died, she said a prayer for him as she normally did before she left. When she finished, Daddy immediately began praying for her and all of us in the room, my two sisters and I. It was the most beautiful prayer I have ever heard, and I felt it was a blessing for us that came through him. I got tears in my eyes as he prayed for himself and us to be "worthy." After she left he said more prayers with one of my sisters, which she also said were beautiful. We all wanted the minister to relate her experience during the funeral. She had never had anyone turn around and pray for her, especially anyone who was dying.

A friend of mine who has worked with dying people for years told me that toward the end of the death process, people reach a "state of grace" in which they say the most beautiful things as though they were coming directly from God. I feel that Daddy was in this state when he said the prayers. I would have had a tape recorder at the hospital had I known this in advance.

When Daddy was in this "state of grace," had I known there was such a thing, I would have had a list of specific questions to ask, such as: "Is there anything you want to tell me or want me to know before you die?" and "What is the most important thing for me to focus on in my life after you die?" I feel this would have been an important opportunity to obtain information, which could be tremendously enlightening and helpful.

When I visited with Daddy I also asked him about his night and day dreams and how he felt about them. Sometimes he would tell me they weren't too clear and other times he would have specific people in them. Some were revealing to me about his inner life.

The day before Daddy died, Mother did not come to the hospital. Exhausted, she decided to stay home to rest and relax all day. I found the coincidence of her staying at home and Daddy's extreme restlessness all day in "Divine Order." It would have upset Mother terribly to see Daddy trying to get up, wanting to go home, and to listen to him talk, moving from subject to subject without coherency.

For me that was another signal that Daddy was going to die because Mother would rarely leave him even to get something to eat, preferring to eat in the room with him. Again, I marveled at the order of the death process and how everyone was just where they would be the most comfortable within themselves. Perfectly timed, this was a loving ordinary miracle for everyone.

I recommend the following actions as they made it so much easier and created deeply meaningful memories I will cherish forever.

- Assist the dying
- Observe each event
- Focus on physical signs
- Prepare and ask questions
- Accept your role
- Celebrate the process

# CHAPTER 4
# Pre-funeral Preparations

One of the things I noticed was the time that Daddy died – 8:35 in the morning. In his usual considerate manner, he died early so we would have the day to adjust and begin preparations for his funeral. Most of our family have been "morning" people all our lives, so he knew we would be dressed and ready for the day by then.

After the mortician came for Daddy's body, I went to the folks' house. When I walked in, the energy in the house felt so different to me. Knowing Daddy would not be there to happily and warmly greet me impacted my "conscious awareness." A few days before I had gone to the folks' house from the hospital during the day when no one was there. When I walked in the silence brought up a deep sadness. I felt that he would never be going back to his home, and I spent some time just walking around, touching his things, and crying for myself and for him. The day he died, the impact on my consciousness was one of acceptance; I said to myself, well, he's gone, life has to go on, and I must just take care of what needs to be done now in this moment. And that is what I did.

Immediately people began arriving and the phone rang constantly when we weren't talking on it. We began the process of calling all of those who were the most distant first then those closer. There were so many people everywhere to call that it took most of the day. Barbara or I would call, introduce ourselves, then tell the person on the other end that Daddy had died, when and where the funeral would be, and that we had a number of other calls to make so we needed to go. Being on the receiving end of the numerous expressions of condolence filled my heart with the love and respect people had for Daddy.

About midway through the day, I took Mother to the funeral home, and we went over the arrangements, picked out the casket within the price range of their plan package, and also picked out the bulletin cover to be passed out to those at the service. I brought along the poem that I had rewritten for Daddy, and it was put on the inside cover of the bulletin. The only things that had to be paid for in the whole funeral were the copies of the death certificates and the tax, which totaled a little over $200. If the plan had not been prepaid, it would have been close to $7,000 for everything. "Plan ahead" took on a new meaning for me. I felt a rightness about preparing my contribution of the photo, poem, and obituary ahead, and supporting Mother at the funeral home.

Later that afternoon Daddy's body was available for viewing, from 1-3 p.m. for the family and from 3- 8 p.m. for everyone else. Mother, Bill, and I visited during the family time as Mother wanted to be sure he looked all right and that his clothes were clean. I chuckled to myself as she found a spot on his suit and I put some spit on my finger and rubbed it out. She kept Daddy's clothes immaculate and spots were immediately removed. There is "Divine" humor everywhere if you recognize and acknowledge it.

Some years before, Bill and I had taken Daddy down to a big and tall men's shop in Los Angeles and bought him a suit. This beautiful suit was black with a fine red weave running through the cloth. He loved how it looked on him, and so did we. I "knew" when we picked it out that it was the suit for Daddy's funeral. I never said anything to him, but when he was telling me what he wanted to wear to his funeral, he picked out this suit, along with a white shirt, a black tie, and his church elder pin for his lapel. The validating of my "knowing" years ago gave me a deep feeling of satisfaction. This was another example, for me, of the importance of "conscious awareness" in advance preparation.

We returned from the funeral home, continued making and receiving calls and began preparations for serving dinner to family members who felt like eating. Food began arriving shortly after the church was notified of Daddy's death, and we had a steady flow of wonderful, delicious, well-rounded dishes. The love with which each food item was prepared was evident in the appearance as well as in the taste.

Their friends' marvelous generosity was apparent in the offers to do any and all they could for us. The openhearted love that people showered on us was another of the joyful gifts of Daddy's death we received. All the words of comfort, the hugs, the cards, the flowers, the food, and the donations filled my heart. Observing the way people showed their love to Mother and my sisters was also enlightening. I watched as the various people gravitated to one sister or the other. It was interesting to observe the connections with each sister. When I am in situations such as this, and in life in general, I seem to have the ability to be in the situation and yet have an overview of it at the same time. Since I live in California, I do not have as close a connection with the majority of people as do my two sisters who live close. This gave me the opportunity to have my own experience as well as share their experience through observation. They are each so different, drawn to different people, and, yet, so alike in their ability to love. Listening to my sisters share some of their experience of Daddy's death revealed to me more clearly some parts of each of them I had not known.

Bill arrived the evening before the funeral and brought the comfort of his protective energy to surround me. Having the person beside me who shared my experiences with Daddy and knew the tenderness of my heart gave me a place to privately express my sorrow and be comforted. I would go to sleep in his arms crying and wake up crying, but during the day I was fine. Each of us has our own way of grieving, and I am extremely private about my innermost feelings, so I was comfortable with this. Occasionally during the day, I would get tears in my eyes.

Our daughters and son arrived Wednesday evening and our family unit was then complete, which meant my heart was happy and at peace. They had called during the days prior to Daddy's death to see how he was and to talk with me, but having them beside me now was deeply comforting for me. The love they gave Bill and me meant so much. They are each very sensitive in different ways and we loved receiving their different expressions of love and support. There are many moments in my life that I tuck away in my heart as special blessings; and their presence is one of these moments.

There is another person who made this time one of joy for me, and that is my dear friend, Shirley, who also happens to be a licensed minister with extensive experience of working with the dying. We met at a women's spiritual group, began working together, and then became friends. When I first told her about Daddy, she gave me ideas about how to begin grieving before Daddy died. She called me several times and opened her heart by allowing me to call her any time of the day or night I needed to talk. Her genuine caring and spiritual knowledge significantly eased this time for me. I have asked God to shower her with infinite blessings, as I know that she does this for many people. I created this friendship for myself with a person who has the same interest in spiritual knowledge and who knew about the death process. I believe I met Shirley to expand my spiritual knowledge, and to deepen my knowledge and acceptance of the death process as part of my important advance preparation.

The next day was filled with more of the same, and that evening we invited all of the relatives who had arrived to eat with us. Mother's two-car garage is carpeted, so Bill and I set up tables and chairs to accommodate the large number of people who were arriving and also to keep the house somewhat quiet. One of the many joys of Daddy's death was visiting with our many relatives and friends that we only see on rare occasions. We had a wonderful time visiting and sharing our memories. We learned some things we had not known about Daddy and about his life, which made it fun and interesting. It seems he was quite spirited as a young man, which gave me a greater sense of connection with Daddy because I am quite spirited myself.

———————————

I recommend the following as these opened up avenues of love and information.

- Notice details
- Observe people
- Initiate things you want
- Find a "death friend"
- Walk beside survivors
- Appreciate family and friends
- Enjoy your own heart

# CHAPTER 5
# A Unique Funeral

My father was quietly very thorough about his life and took care of things so his family didn't have to worry. He and Mother had purchased two crypts at Memorial Gardens Cemetery and Mausoleum, where he and Mother planned to be entombed after they died. He had paid for everything many years before. About a year before Daddy died, Barbara and I checked on everything just to be sure expenses were covered. There were no problems and everything was in place. Making sure that burial and funeral arrangements were planned and paid for in advance gave me freedom from concern about financial matters when either of the folks died. I didn't have to worry about selecting a plot and all the financial details at the last moment. What a wonderful example they gave me for my own life planning.

A few years before that I sat down with the folks and asked them what they wanted in the way of a funeral. I wanted to do this so I could put it all down on paper. I suspected that at the time each died I might not be in a place emotionally to think clearly. I wanted to be certain of their desires and that they would be honored. I asked them about the following for their funeral service. This was what Daddy wanted:

**Location:** He wanted his funeral service held in the church that he had attended for 37 years.

**Presiding Officials:** Daddy wanted to have the current and past ministers conduct the service together. The other members of my family and I elected to include a third minister who had the deeply moving personal experience praying with Daddy the day before he died.

**Casket:** Daddy wanted an open casket in the church parlor before the service and wanted it closed, then moved to the front of the church sanctuary during the service.

**Pall Bearers:** Daddy said to have Mother do whatever she wanted about pall bearers. We decided to have the mortuary personnel move the casket from the parlor to the front of the church and then on to the cemetery. There were so many people who considered themselves my father's best friends that we didn't want anyone's feelings hurt.

**Music:** Daddy wanted the song "Finlandia" sung by the congregation and then some music that wasn't "screeching." I brought with me a taped version of "In This Very Room" which we asked a couple to sing. The woman was the church choir director. Daddy's nephew, Louis, a gifted pianist, played the most moving version of "Just a Closer Walk With Thee." The church organist, a friend of the folks, played the organ.

**Service Program Bulletin:** This bulletin outlined the funeral service, contained Daddy's life obituary, and the poem I rewrote entitled "Faded Blue Overalls."

**Tape Record and/or Video:** The service was tape recorded, and we were given a master copy of the tape. No video service was offered and we did not choose to have it done. I was deeply grateful for the cassette tape of the service as during the service I was not able to concentrate on much that was said. I heard the words but did not retain them. Now, when I listen to it, I hear something more each time and appreciate the beauty of the service. After I returned home, I made copies of the tape and sent them to members of my immediate family as well as those people who were close to Daddy who had been unable to attend, or we felt would want to hear the service.

**Pictures:** Just after the family sat in the church pew, I took pictures of the family, the flowers, and the casket in the front of the church. After the service, Wayne, our son took pictures of family members and others we didn't usually see. Bill ran out of film the evening before, but Daddy had left some in the refrigerator so Mother told him to use that. When we got them back from the developers, they were black and white. I thought that was ironic and symbolic of the occasion. I thought "Divine" humor was at work again.

**Flowers:** Daddy requested donations in lieu of flowers. Every special occasion for years Daddy would give Mother or the entire family red roses. It was very important to Mother to cover his casket with red roses.

**Donations:** Daddy wanted donations to go to a home for abused children and to his church.

**Transportation:** Part of the funeral package that the folks had paid for included two limousines from home to the church, to the cemetery, then back home. Relatives took care of other transportation arrangements as the need arose.

**Child Care:** The day before we had asked if there would be child care and were told they would try to arrange for it. We have a two-year-old granddaughter we knew would be better off in child care. No arrangements had been made when we arrived at the church, and I quickly arranged for a volunteer woman to care for her. Because I did this, I missed being present when the minister gave a prayer for all of us just prior to our being led down the aisle. I have the mindset that everything works out for the best so I thought it was clear I did not need to hear that prayer.

**Luncheon Buffet:** The church women prepared a delicious luncheon for the immediate family and friends (around 100 people) after the service. Mother initially suggested having it catered, but one of the ministers volunteered that the church women normally did this in honor of the family. Mother had done this for other church families for years, now it was her turn to receive.

The day before the funeral the main minister asked to get together with all available members of our immediate family, to talk with us about our feelings for Daddy, which the minister found helped with the grieving process. He told us he was treating the service as a celebration of Daddy's life. He said that sometimes people present one face to the minister and another to their family. He wanted to know the face Daddy presented to the family. Of course, in Daddy's case they were the same.

We told him that Daddy was a genuine person, loved his family, his farm, all of humanity, and he especially loved God. Daddy was an international business man having traveled all over the world on behalf of the wheat organization. He also sponsored people from other countries. The minister asked each of us our earliest memories of Daddy and one word to describe him. When it came my turn, I burst into tears and things came out that I had buried about my deep love for him. Some of the things surprised even me. Afterward, I felt such a free openness surrounding me - that same lightness that I normally feel after strong emotions are released. If I had not done all of the advance emotional grieving work, I probably would have skipped talking with the minister because I wouldn't have wanted to expose my deeper feelings.

Thursday, October 8, 1998, dawned a clear and bright sunny day. I knew in my heart it would be just as Daddy wanted- a day that was glorious to celebrate his leaving. All the family arrived at the church ahead of the others attending and went into the parlor to view Daddy's body. There were many more bouquets of flowers than at the funeral home. Someone commented that Daddy didn't look right without his glasses, and I said to myself that I really didn't expect him to look right, period. I chuckled to myself that people would notice and mention that. Humor abounds everywhere if you look for it.

This was only the second funeral I had ever attended, so the procedures of the day were interesting to me. The first funeral I attended was on a much smaller scale. Being part of the funeral versus attending makes a considerable difference. The family was instructed to remain in the parlor and told they would be escorted down front after everyone else was seated. As I returned from arranging child care for our granddaughter, the family was lining up to go down the aisle. I was struck by the similarity between a wedding and a funeral. Daddy gave me away and now I was giving him away.

The service was beautiful and each individual person's part added just the right touch. I had arranged with the main minister to speak after the last song, if I felt I could. The arrangement was that I would walk to the podium if I could speak and, if not, he would continue with the closing. I had made a promise to Daddy to do certain things for him, and I knew I would keep that promise. So, I walked to the podium and with heartfelt emotion said the following (edited):

*I'm the surprise – to me, too. While we were in the hospital I was with Dad a lot, and there were a couple of words that were important to him. The nurses would come in to turn Dad and they would hurt him a great deal. He would call them the pain crew. After they finished every single thing, he would say: "Thank you." I'm kind of a messenger for him; he asked me to say and do some things for him if I could:*

*Thank you for coming, thank you for giving Dad and us your love and support.*

*Thank you, Aunt Helen and Aunt Fern, for the wonderful Saturday morning conversations on the phone, for the letters you wrote to him that he loved so much.*

*Mother, thank you for the years of loving care when it was very, very difficult for you to do things when he wasn't at his best.*

*Barbara (my sister). Every family has an 'Earth Angel.' Barbara is our 'Earth Angel.' These are people who quietly go about doing what needs to be done. I mean the daily cooking, running errands, taking care of business things. Barbara is our 'Earth Angel', and she took care of things for the folks. Barbara, thank you so much.*

*Dan (Barbara's husband), thank you for your advice, for your humor.*

*Pat (my sister), and Daryl and Lee Ann (her children), thank you for your tremendous emotional, loving support. Dad always felt your love so much.*

*Louis (Dad's nephew and my cousin) is the fellow who played the piano and Dad considered him a stand-in son and he wanted to thank you, Louis.*

*Bill (my precious husband) for all the years that you have said yes to coming back here, instead of going someplace else, for every vacation we spent here. Thank you so much, for loving Dad that much.*

*And (to myself), thank you, Nancy, for being able to get up here to speak.*

*And last, but by no means least, thank you, Dad, for a wonderful, wonderful life."*

I cannot describe the feeling of joy I gave myself by speaking to those in attendance. I didn't realize until after I had listened to the tape a couple of times that the audience in this traditional protestant church clapped for me after I finished. I still get a deep feeling of intense gratification when I remember it.

Our family formed a receiving line afterward and numerous people commented on how unique and beautiful the service was. It reminded me of a wedding receiving line. One woman in the line said to me: "Your Dad would have been proud of you." Her words brought tears to my eyes. I felt it was a message from Daddy.

I would not have missed giving myself all of these healing, joyful gifts for anything.

We had a delicious luncheon and then the immediate family went to the mausoleum where the casket had been placed before the open crypt. Two cushioned benches were placed in front of the casket where Mother and those needing to sit were taken. I took some more pictures - black and white (smile). The minister said a few more words and a prayer, then we returned to Mother's house. I noticed that I no longer thought of it as the "folks' house." Some shifts in consciousness come fairly quickly and easily for me; another insight into becoming "aware" in advance.

The immediate family came over to the house, and we again had dinner and visited. This time everyone was much more joyful, and there was an ease in conversations and even more laughter than on the previous evening.

---

These recommendations saved me untold hours, days, and weeks of agony, and truly helped make his funeral a joyful miracle.

- Make and pay for funeral or cremation arrangements ahead of time
- Participate in the funeral
- Receive the love offered
- Participate in all activities
- Check cameras and film
- Listen for the silent messages

## CHAPTER 6
# Going On Without Daddy

Daddy's body was entombed. His spirit was free, and life goes on. What a difference a day makes.

The day after the funeral we began the process of going on without Daddy. I am a person who believes in doing things now, not later. Mother, my sisters, and I scheduled a corporation meeting at 9 a.m. the day after the funeral to elect new officers and take care of corporation business. Afterward, we discussed and started a list of the other things that needed to be done in the days and weeks following.

The first thing we did was clean out Daddy's things from his closet and drawers. Mother wanted all of us to do it while we were there and get whatever we wanted of his. I loved going through Daddy's things. I found cards he had saved that my sisters and I had given him as well as gifts we had sent. I got a sense of what really meant something to him and how deeply he treasured the things of the heart. I found several little books of blank note paper which I took and samples of things that were useful he'd saved to use rather than buy new. These simple things reflected to me how important he felt it was to just concentrate on the love, rather than material things.

My cousin had asked for something of Daddy's for himself, and the idea came to send all of the cousins on Daddy's side something of his. Mother thought this was a wonderful idea. I selected the things I thought would mean something to each of them and then went over each item with Mother. I wanted to be sure that nothing was given away that she wanted. Bill and I boxed the things up, then took them to be mailed that day. This touched those who received them a great deal and gave me a wonderful feeling that I was instrumental in seeing that the love Daddy felt for them was expressed in yet another way.

I found it very important to complete each thing and, if possible, not to leave it to do the next day. I enjoy having each day be complete unto itself, so when I wake up tomorrow it is brand new with nothing left from yesterday. It's like having a brand-new piece of paper on which to paint the day's picture or write the day's story.

The things no one wanted we placed in the garage for a neighbor to pick up and take to a second-hand store that Daddy had designated he wanted what was left of his things to go to. There were things Mother didn't know what to do with, and I suggested she wait until she did know. I didn't want her to hurry removing things that she was not sure about. I know for myself when I am not sure about something, I do nothing until I "know" for sure.

The next thing we did was move Mother's things to fill in the empty space in the closet. Things had to be carried from downstairs to the upstairs. This served to save her some steps as well as get her somewhat excited about having all of her clothes in one place. I felt so proud of my children as they carried load after load of clothes upstairs, allowing themselves to fully participate in helping to heal Mother's life in that way.

Our children had to fly back to their homes Saturday, and others who had driven began their trips home also. The following day, we decided to write thank you notes while we listened to the cassette tape of the funeral service and my cousin's Romantic Piano Classics tape. Bill folded the thank you notes, I addressed the envelopes, and Mother wrote the notes. We had a lovely day as we seemed to be in such a soft place in our hearts. Realizing all of the love that people felt for Daddy and us gave the day a glow. We completed all of the thank you notes that day. I was so glad I had made the master thank you note on my computer so that all we had to do was have copies made on paper of Mother's choice and buy envelopes.

Monday was a legal holiday, so we could not take care of any business and we rested. It seemed to me that also was in "Divine Order," an additional day of rest. Bill was returning to our home in Northern California the next day and I made the decision to fly back with him as I was exhausted. The remainder of the tasks would take considerably more time and needed to be done by Barbara who was the executor of Daddy's estate. I was very sad to leave Mother at the airport the next morning, and we both cried as we knew each of our lives was changed forever without Daddy's presence.

We flew into Sacramento and then drove to our home. When we stepped off the plane in Sacramento, I was struck by the difference in energy between Colorado and California. The energy felt so much lighter in Sacramento, and both Bill and I noted the difference. It was gratifying to have Bill notice subtle changes in energy also.

For a couple of weeks after we returned home, we did nothing but rest and handle what was absolutely required of us. One of the things that required our attention was our motor home that we put for sale on consignment. The motor home was sold, given to the people who bought it, and we were not paid for it. The consignment people took our money and would not pay us. The people who bought the motor home would not give it back. We had to go to court to get the motor home and some of the money back. We found that this served to focus our thoughts off Daddy and onto dealing with this present situation. It was something that could not be ignored and required us to take some action or make some decision every single day. While it was initially upsetting, I can see the purpose in it now and chuckle at the "Divine" humor in saying to us: "We are not going to let you sit and be sad; we are going to keep you busy doing our work."

The motor home problem was eventually resolved, and I think Daddy helped smooth the way. Spirit used us to see that the consignment couple was arrested, convicted and had to reimburse every person they had been stealing from. The people who had the motor home lost all the money they had paid and were forced to turn it over to the bank that held our loan. The consignment people had been doing this for a long time to older people who could not fight for themselves. Because of my career background of building cases for problem personnel for the federal government, I kept detailed notes of every word said by the consignment people and myself or Bill. I typed up a detailed chronology and turned it over to the Sheriff's Department. It was instrumental in getting them arrested and convicted.

Once in a while Bill and I would get tears in our eyes as we recalled those parts of our life with Daddy that we miss. Some mornings I wake up with the thought in my mind "Good morning, Sweetie," and I feel Daddy greeting me.

My birthday is November 12 and our wedding anniversary was the 23rd of November, so we made the decision to begin celebrating early. I started my birthday celebrations with my first party on November 4. We began planning to throw ourselves a wonderful wedding anniversary party. We both felt Daddy would want us to celebrate because he was proud of our marriage and loved parties.

Once we made the decision to start celebrating, our hearts lightened and we started feeling more joyful. The planning and preparation for these events kept us busy and excited.

———————

I recommend the following to assist the survivors, keep yourself moving forward, and gift others.

- Do it now
- Clean out personal items

- Mail relatives surprise keepsakes
- Write thank you notes together
- Create survivor's new space
- Leave when you need to
- Be mindful of the need to change focus to the present
- Enjoy Divine humor
- Celebrate your life

## CHAPTER 7
# Memories of One Year After Dad's Death

The following is what I wrote one year after Dad's death.

*Today is October 6, 1999, one year since Daddy died. My life has changed in so many ways and, yet, it hasn't changed at all. I see his hand and God's hand in all of it more clearly.*

*I have been praying for rain for weeks because of the fires here in Northern California; this morning when I awakened, Bill told me it was raining. I thanked Daddy and God as I feel this was his way of blessing me and the earth, acknowledging this special day when he left his physical body, with a clearing rain. I meditated then listened to the tape of his funeral and recalled the day he left.*

*I carry the inheritance of the love of God, the farm, and my family within the cells of my physical body. I had envisioned carrying this inheritance forward physically, mentally, emotionally, and spiritually by assisting in the management of the farm and the corporation. When Daddy's beloved farm was sold and I received the check in partial payment for my shares, the reality of the loss of all he created deeply affected me. It was such a sacred part of my life.*

*I am releasing the loss layer by layer, and as I let go, I feel a lightness and new directions begin to come into focus. As with Daddy's death, funeral, and burial, I feel a joyful inner calm and peaceful acceptance. I am freeing myself in ways I did not know I needed to be freed. Old ways, feelings, thoughts and ideas are dying and new ones are being born.*

*One of the ways I reviewed myself during this year was to write letters to myself. I would begin with "Dear Changing Woman:" and then describe the ways in which I changed and why. This was an insightful journey into how I used to be and how I am now. A memory surfaced about when I won a beauty contest in my twenties and how beautiful I felt my body was. Along with that memory came the awareness of how much I had valued outer beauty at that time and what others thought of me. The difference in the inner beauty I feel within myself now, is far more meaningful to me than any outer beauty recognition I am given by others. Genuinely liking myself, living passionately, and acknowledging the importance of my own inner beauty is honoring the God-given part of me.*

*I found another very effective way for me to gain greater "conscious awareness" within myself was to join an Art Expression Class at the local college. Twice a week, I draw for three hours and write whatever comes to mind after each drawing. This has opened a deeper level of creativity within me, as well as being a forum for the expression of my feelings. What I was unable to express with words, I was able to express through my drawing first and then through my writing afterwards. This is a powerful process and one I strongly recommend.*

*I completed and paid for my own final arrangements during this year. I feel a sense of peace now that I am ready when it is time for my physical body to die.*

*My friend's mother was dying, so she invited her family for a get-together, and then her friends to a tea to select keepsakes to remember her by after she was gone. I think this is a lovely idea and decided I will do this also as it feels like a warm way to share things I love.*

*Daddy taught me to love first a single seed, then a field of golden, ripe wheat, a dog, a cat, the clouds, a sunset, old people, the world. His world was love - for himself and for all God created. This is the inheritance I shall carry forward.*

*Daddy's death marked the beginning of my surrender to my own path. I honor the things he taught me about love, integrity, ethics, honesty, tradition, nature, and God. It is as though I knew that when he died, I would be going in a different direction from the one I followed when he was alive. In some way, his death freed me from many things and opened my heart in a greater, deeper way. I am so grateful for each "awareness."*

*I am less than I was because he is not here to share the part of me that belonged to him alone. Yet, I am more than I was because that part is freed up to share with Bill, our family, and the world - that unique ability to radiate love from my Soul. It is a different love, richer, fuller, more discerning.*

*I will do my best to pass on his legacy of love to my family. I leave them free to choose whatever path they want for themselves and trust that God will lead them to their greater good like I am being lead to mine.*

*A part of my heart will forever hold the precious love of my father, my friend, and my farm partner in treasured memory. This is my own joyful miracle. I wish each of you the same.*

_____

Give yourself the gift of allowing the death process inside yourself to be a joyful miracle. I recommend the following.

- Believe in miracles
- Let go and change
- Meditate daily
- Review your life
- Surrender to your path

- Indulge your creative Spirit
- Live passionately in this moment
- Accept your own splendor
- Create and live your legacy
- Cherish precious memories

**CHAPTER 8**
# Suggested Death Check List

**Do these things now or as soon as possible:**

_____ Establish revocable living trust, and/or review or make will now

_____ Purchase complete death package (cemetery plot, crypt, cremation)

_____ Write a list of everything you want in your Celebration of Life service or funeral

_____ Write obituary of main life events (you can always update it)

_____ Make, or review, a list of mail addresses, email addresses, and phone numbers (review yearly to update)

_____ Save a good picture

**Do these things when death is imminent:**

_____ Notify family and friends of pending or actual death

_____ Meet with mortuary representative

_____ Pay costs at end of meeting

_____ Write short obituary for newspaper(s)

**Do these things as soon as a person dies:**

_____ Select casket or cremation urn (ask family if they want a token jewelry item with ashes in it)

_____ Ascertain where ashes are to be placed (garden, ocean, mountains, etc.)

_____ Casket location and open or closed

_____ Select brochure cover and contents (service outline, poems, life obituary, photos)

_____ Set times for family and public viewing of body, if appropriate

_____ Determine number of death certificates needed (order more than you think you will need as we found every business/company/policy wanted an original copy and they are cheaper if you order all at once)

_____ Plan funeral or Celebration of Life

_____ Decide on date and time

_____ Funeral or Celebration of Life Service location (Church, cemetery or elsewhere)

_____ Presiding official(s)

_____ Pall bearers (How many or none)

_____ Music (vocal/organ/piano/instrumental)

_____ Choose poem, sayings, or scripture favorites

_____ Tape record or video

_____ Pictures (check camera, film and batteries)

_____ Determine if immediate family member(s) or friend(s) want to speak at service

_____ Flowers (identify type and color preference, if any)

_____ Donations (name(s) and addresses of organizations)

_____ Transportation (home to church, church to cemetery, back to home, or none)

_____ Child care

_____ Handicapped needs

_____ Meal afterward (donated or catered or none)

## Do these things after the service and the days following:

_____ Plan following days' activities (make lists)

_____ Determine survivor's desires

_____ Make business decisions

_____ Notify executor, if appropriate

_____ Remove belongings of deceased, if requested

_____ Arrange for or take things to be donated

_____ Ask if close relatives or friends want anything of deceased

_____ Select and disperse Items for giving or mailing to close relatives or friends

_____ Write thank you notes

_____ Assist with rearranging clothes or furniture, if survivor desires

_____ Rest periodically

_____ Plan little and big celebrations

_____ Contact burial organization for flower and visitation rules

**Do these things during the weeks following:**

_____ Review trust or will

_____ Review financial status (loans, bills, savings, checking, safe deposit boxes) (Check for secret hiding places – my husband found $265 cash hidden in a book)

_____ Review all assets owned (personal and property, partnerships, corporations)

_____ Review titles on all property

_____ Review all incoming medical and nonmedical bills and verify before paying

_____ Review paper and computer files

_____ Cancel magazines, newsletters and papers, if appropriate

_____ Contact Social Security Administration

_____ Contact credit card companies for reissue and possible insurance policy

_____ Contact banks and credit unions for account name change and possible insurance policy (most cover accidental death and dismemberment)

_____ Contact life insurance agent

_____ Contact automobile insurance agent

_____ Contact investment broker(s)

_____ Contact previous employer for possible death benefits or survivor's pension

_____ Contact AAA for possible death benefits and any refund due

_____ Change health insurance policy coverage

_____ Check for refunds of subscriptions paid and insurance policy premiums

_____ Reissue traveler's checks in survivor's name

_____ Contact Certified Public Accountant (obtain advice on taxes, property, stocks, and other related matters)

_____ Contact attorney if needed (Certified Public Accountant is usually more economical and knowledgeable)

_____ Contact other agencies (if self-employed or employed by public or private company)

_____ Contact county officials to change title on residence

_____ Contact religious/spiritual organizations to ascertain tithing status

_____ Contact schools or educational organizations

_____ Contact military service organizations

_____ Check for patents pending

_____ Check for legal issues pending

_____ Check guardianship of minor children

_____ Check alimony or child support payments

_____ Cancel retail store credit cards and request reissue to survivor

_____ Cancel passport

Thank yourself for your courage, strength, and great love, for your willingness to do the difficult things, and for just being part of a family. Give yourself a hug!

## CHAPTER 9
# Update

It has been almost seventeen years since I wrote about my father's death, and as I read back over the experience, it was like yesterday. My father continues to communicate with me from the Other Side and occasionally leaves me a penny or pennies. A recent morning when I was out for a walk around 6:00 am, there was a shiny new penny on the sidewalk. I thanked him for it. I felt it was his way of acknowledging that I am updating this book and he is pleased. If I ask him for assistance with anything, it is given. If I ask him to watch over or assist family members, I can see the results of it. If I ask him to help me move further along my path, I am shown the best way for me, and I follow it. I don't miss him anymore as he is here whenever I call.

Much has transpired in my personal life with Bill and I moving from Bella Vista, California to Corvallis, Oregon, for ten years. We co-owned Sacred Healing, LLC, and did healing for people in Oregon, and elsewhere.

After doing everything western medicine, and I, knew how to heal Bill's back pain and walking problems, we went to see John of God in Brazil in 2004 and 2005. For me each trip was a spiritual awakening at a deeper level. John of God is a world-renowned healer. Bill had psychic surgery, was in bed for 24 hours, and spent the time we were there resting and in meditation. His back pain improved to almost nothing and he walked until he died. The most significant change was that he opened spiritually.

When western medicine can do no more, a trip to John of God can change your life. Your physical body may or may not heal completely, but spiritually you have the opportunity to change markedly.

We were guided to move from Corvallis to North Las Vegas, Nevada in 2011 as Bill began having memory issues and we needed to be closer to the children, plus I was concerned about finances if he needed extensive care. I took care of him from 2006 until he left his body June 3, 2014. Those eight years were a spiritual journey of a depth which I am still discovering.

His death changed my inner and outer life in all ways. I sold the home in North Las Vegas and went to live with my son, Wayne, and his wife, Nikki, for a while as I found my way. In May of 2015, I purchased a home in Auburn, California, where I plan to spend the remainder of my life in this realm. My life is full with Spirit embodied in my Beingness now, with my writing, my spiritual journeys to Mount Shasta, Sacred Journey Sessions, Ballroom Dancing, my precious little Reggie dog, and my family and friends.

In early November of 2016, I finished writing *My Spiritual Journey and Yours* about my spiritual journey with my little dog, Reggie. In it I made space for others to create their own spiritual journey. For years I had searched for something simple to follow on my journey, but did not find anything. With the thought of helping others learn and create their own path, I decided to write about my journey.

On November 21, 2016, my heart stopped and I had a pacemaker put in the next morning. I completely left my body and went to the Other Side. It was an exit point for me as I felt I had completed the things that I came to do to that point in my life. On the Other Side, I met with Bill, my mother and father, other family members, pets, friends, The Council, and Source. When I chose to come back I knew I was to write about that journey. The result was *Booked: Trip to the Other Side and Back*. I know with certainty that there is so much more to our lives and journeys than we consciously know. It was imparted to me how important it is to open up to all that Spirit has to offer as life improves in each moment in unimaginable ways if one is willing. Now, I live in Spirit and I am deeply content with my little Reggie and my simple life.

I am writing about the spiritual journey of Bill and I, and our children in another book, as it is a rare and precious gift that we have maintained loving relationships as a step family for almost 50 years. My connection with Bill has replaced the one with my father. My connection with Bill is so deep and close, I feel him with me every day. Sometimes, I feel like he breathes for me. He comes to me not only in thought form, but in physical form every day as a blue bird to bring me happiness and in honor of his years of a Los Angeles Police Officer.

Spirit guides my every thought, word, and action. Thoughts and ideas come into my mind that amaze me. For instance, this morning I needed to make my health drink and had the thought to put some sweet mint in the drink. So, I went on the porch to my little herb garden and was going to cut three or four little leaves like I usually do. Instead, Spirit had me cut two whole stocks of sweet mint which made a big stack of leaves. I put them in my drink along with some fruit, cinnamon, meal shake, and was delighted at the wonderful flavor it gave the drink.

Curious as to why they had me put so much in, I looked up sweet mint online and here is what it said. "Commonly used as a flavoring in beverages and foods, mint is also believed to have medicinal purposes—both as a leaf and as an oil. Peppermint oil is often applied to the skin as a treatment for headaches, muscle and nerve pain, inflammation, and even for repelling mosquitoes. A good source of Vitamins A and C, mint helps with vision and immune functions. The herb is also packed with antioxidants that protect against cell damage, boost the immune system, and form collagen in the body." So, Spirit gave me a boost for my body in the form of a large helping of sweet mint.

This is how each day flows with Spirit. The beauty and grace of my life is a gift I gave myself by opening to Spirit. There is a magic and mystery to it as I never know what is going to flow in as a surprise.

May you give yourself the gift of knowing that "death" is just a transition from one realm to another, that there is nothing to fear, and that the bliss you encounter when you reach the Other Side is worth everything.

May you give yourself the gift of Spirit's guidance and love as you continue on your journey here on Earth.

Always you the human, you the Spirit, are loved beyond measure.

# Acknowledgments

In honor of the deep love given to my father by William (Bill) E Waldron, my deceased husband.

In appreciation of the genuine love, support, and encouragement from family, friends, editors, and publishing companies.

With gratitude to those who made any contribution to this book.

To Sue Crawford, my exceptionally creative and talented friend, editor, cover designer, website manager, book manager, and good business sense person, you are a gift from Spirit. You make it so easy for me to bring forth what Spirit asks, then you make it presentable for the public, and get it distributed. You are a joy to work with and your love for my little Reggie and I, warms both our hearts. Thank you from the bottom of my heart. I love you, my dear friend.

To Spirit, I am eternally grateful for your enfoldment.

# Resources

**Mediums Recommended:**

- Cherry Divine, www.cherrydivine.com
- Debbie Smith, www.debbie-smith.net

**Books:**

- *The Bible*
- *How to Survive the Loss of a Love* by Melba Colgrove, Ph.D., Harold H. Bloomfield, M.D. and Peter McWilliams
- *Hello From Heaven!* By Bill Guggenheim and Judy Guggenheim
- *Talking to Heaven, A Medium's Message of Life After Death* by James Van Praagh
- *To Heaven and Back* by Mary C. Neal, M.D.
- *Stillness Speaks* by Eckhart Tolle
- *The Power of Now* by Eckhart Tolle
- *Same Soul, Many Bodies* by Brian L. Weiss, M.D.
- *Death The Final Stage of Growth* by Elisabeth Kubler-Ross
- *Who Dies?* By Stephen Levine
- *Healing Into Life and Death* by Stephen Levine
- *Embracing the Beloved* by Stephen and Ondrea Levine

**Websites:**

- My website, www.nancyawaldron.com, has other resources listed.

# About the Author

**Nancy A. Waldron** is an author and a spiritual mentor who facilitates Sacred Journey Workshops, Sacred Journey Sessions, and Mount Shasta Spiritual Journeys. She is a conduit for Light from the Other Side to assist humanity in increasing its energy, vibration, and frequency.

Nancy was born multi-gifted, and at a young age dedicated her life to the continuous opening to Spirit and to mentoring others. She considers she has a PhD in her personal life experience, both the good and not so

*Nancy Waldron and Reggie*

good. Her journey took her through therapy, churches, psychics, and healers, as well as a life-long study of spirituality through *The Bible*, many other books, classes, workshops, retreats, and individual sessions with spiritual leaders. This process led her to decide to publicly share her innate spiritual knowing.

She co-owned Sacred Healing, LLC, in Oregon, with her (deceased) husband, facilitating healing of people and situations in the United States and elsewhere. They facilitated individual healing, and hosted weekly meditation groups and Sacred Healing Circles. She works with people remotely by viewing a photograph, by telephone, in groups, and in person.

# Other Books by Nancy A Waldron

*A Joyful Miracle*, published in 2000 and updated in 2017, was written following her father's death and after her first trip to the Other Side. It describes her spiritual and practical preparation prior to her father's death, as well as her actions during and after his death. It provides suggestions at the end of each chapter and a Suggested Death Checklist for others to follow.

*My Spiritual Journey and Yours* was written just prior to her second trip to the Other Side and published in December 2016. It tells about how she, with the help of her little dog, Reggie, brings Spirit into her life every moment of every day. She believes everything is in Divine Order – not her order. She shares information on how she creates: My Sacred Space, My Body, My Garden Play, My Porch Time, Situation Techniques, Prayers Along the Way, My Reminders Along the Way, Self Talk, Sex, The Environment, and the gratitude that fills all. There is space for you to create your own spiritual journey in each section of the book.

*BOOKED: Trip to the Other Side and Back*, published in 2017, was written after her second trip to the Other Side. In it she tells about her experiences before, during, and after her two trips to the Other side. She completely crossed over to the Other Side for the second time, merged with family, friends, pets, The Council, and Source while on the Other Side. Her physical body was worked on by Interstellar Surgeons and Light Beings as well as the nurses and medical doctors in the Emergency Room here on Earth. She shares her journey before, during, and after she came back into her body.

She is currently writing about her experiences with her husband and children as a stepfamily. Watch for other books by Nancy.

Nancy's books are available at:
www.amazon.com
www.CreateSpace.com

Or directly from the author:
530.878.5757 | nancyawaldron@aol.com
Checks and credit cards are accepted

Every Moment

of

Every Day

is

Sacred

Reggie

*9 7 8 0 9 9 8 8 3 8 3 2 8 *